How Do I Find Information Online?

Tricia Yearling

How Do I Find Information Online?

Online Smarts

Tricia Yearling

Enslow Publishing
101 W. 23rd Street
Suite 240
New York, NY 10011
USA

enslow.com

Words to Know

encyclopedia—A print or online database with information about many subjects.

experts—People who know a lot about a subject.

keywords—Important words that are used in a search.

links—Words that are highlighted on a Web page that take you to other Web pages when you click on them.

network—A group of connected computers.

preferences—The choices people make about a computer's setup.

search engine—Software that finds Web pages, documents, and files on the Internet.

source—Something that gives facts or knowledge.

subscription—An agreement to receive and to pay for something.

topic—The subject of a piece of writing.

Contents

Words to Know 4

Chapter 1: What Is Research? 7

Chapter 2: Starting Your Research 12

Chapter 3: Starting With the Source 16

Chapter 4: Choose Carefully 20

Chapter 5: Become an Expert Researcher 26

Learn More 30

Index 31

What Is Research?

Have you ever looked up the words to a song online? Do you use the Internet to find your favorite show on YouTube? Do you look for photos of cute baby animals? If you have, then you have done Internet research!

Internet research means looking for information online. Searching for songs or pictures online is a form of Internet research. Looking up facts online for school reports is Internet research too. The Internet is a great tool

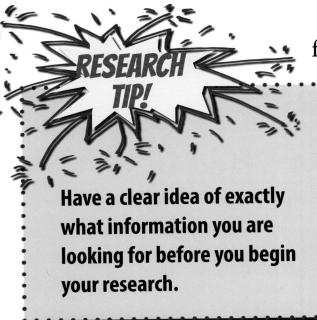

RESEARCH TIP!

Have a clear idea of exactly what information you are looking for before you begin your research.

for getting information. To find something online, though, you have to know what you are looking for. You also have to know how to find it. Knowing how to do online research can help you learn about anything that interests you, from how to make lemonade to what team scored the most touchdowns in the Superbowl.

The World Wide Web

The World Wide Web is a **network** made up of all the Web sites on the Internet. This makes it a powerful tool. Web sites can give both the history of a **topic** and the latest news. For example, you can read about recent events at the White House and learn about all the past presidents of the United States at kids.usa.gov.

While many sites on the Internet can be used for research, not everything you read online is

This screen capture shows the home page of the kids.usa.gov Web site. There are many Web pages on different topics.

RESEARCH TIP!

If you are unsure whether you can trust the information on a site, ask your teacher before you use facts from the site in a report.

true. Some sites, such as blogs or personal Web sites, list people's opinions rather than facts. Other sites belong to companies for which it is more important to sell you something than it is to give you accurate information.

Make sure a Web site is a reliable **source** before you trust the information on it. Web sites created by museums or government organizations are reliable sources. They post information written and reviewed by **experts**. Web sites created by companies or individuals are not reliable sources. They may contain information that is an opinion, incorrect, or misleading.

Starting Your Research

The best place to start your online research is by using a search engine. A **search engine** is software that checks millions of Web sites for words you ask it to find. Then it lists Web sites that use those words. There are many search engines. Some popular search engines are Google and Kids Click. Sometimes using different search engines gives you different results.

Try one of the search engines listed here. Ask an adult to use search-engine **preferences** to block sites that are not safe for kids. Then try some searches to see which search engines give you the best results. The best results list sites that give you the information you are looking for.

Choosing Good Keywords

Search engines look only for what you ask them to find. This makes choosing the best **keywords** very important. A keyword is a word or concept that is important in your research. When choosing your keywords, think about exactly what you want to know.

Say you want to learn about how caterpillars

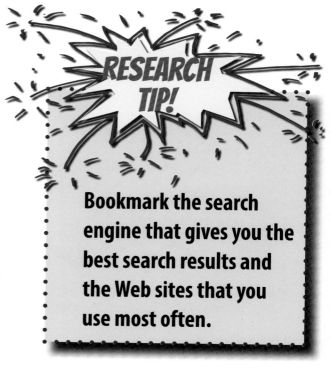

RESEARCH TIP!

Bookmark the search engine that gives you the best search results and the Web sites that you use most often.

become butterflies. A search for "caterpillar" will get more than a million results. Every Web site with the word "caterpillar" will show up, even songs or books that include the word "caterpillar." It can be difficult to find what you want if you have to sort through so many sites. Instead, try a search for the keywords "caterpillar becomes butterfly." This will narrow down the number of Web sites to just those that have that information on them. It will be much easier for you to find what you need if you only have to look at a few sites.

RESEARCH TIP!

If you want to find words in an exact order, place keywords in quotation marks when you are doing a search.

When searching for keywords, be as specific as possible so you get the information you want.

Starting With the Source

One of the best places to find information is by going to the source. A source can be a person or a group or an organization that specializes in the information that you want. Web sites created by zoos or natural history museums can be great sources of information on animals or habitats. To learn about space exploration, try NASA's Web site. For information on American history, visit the Smithsonian Institute's National Museum of American History.

Some sites, like that of the Field Museum in Chicago, have experts to whom you can e-mail questions. Always check with your teacher, mother, father, or guardian before e-mailing someone you do not know. If you get an e-mail back from an expert, remember to say thank you.

A dinosaur skeleton stands outside the Field Museum of Natural History. You can e-mail experts through the museum's Web site.

Researching Closer to Home

There may be times when your first stop in doing Internet research will be your online classroom. Does your class or school have a Web site? If it does, use it. Ask your teacher or librarian what kinds of things you can find on the site. You may be able to use it to find reading lists or homework. Your teacher or librarian may have set up **links** to other useful sites for you to use too.

Find out if your school or library has a **subscription** to an online **encyclopedia**, such as www. worldbookonline. com or www. britannica.com. These sites have articles written by

RESEARCH TIP!

Keep a list of good sites to use for research.

experts. Online encyclopedias let you search many topics, such as science, art, and social studies.

RESEARCH TIP!

Librarians can help you do research both online and using books.

Choose Carefully

When you search for information online, you will find many different kinds of Web sites. Some sites give people's opinions. Other sites are meant to make people laugh, not to supply information. Some sites even have false information.

A Web site's address offers clues to its research value. You can usually trust government sites, which end in ".gov" and school sites, which end in ".edu." Sites ending in ".org" may or may not be useful. For example, the site of the American

Museum of Natural History, www.amnh.org, is a great source. But the site www.wikipedia.org should not be used for schoolwork. This site has up-to-date information, but anybody can add to it. Sometimes this site contains mistakes, jokes, or incorrect information.

The American Museum of Natural History's Web site has a page that breaks information down by grade level.

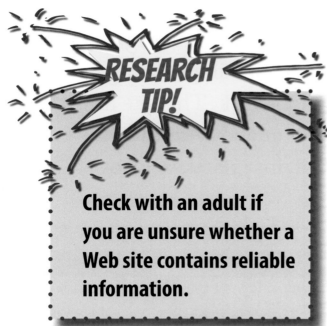

RESEARCH TIP!

Check with an adult if you are unsure whether a Web site contains reliable information.

Can You Trust It?

Web sites that sell things are not reliable sources of information. People who make these Web sites want to make money, not supply information. Sites ending in ".com" are often run by companies or people who want you to buy something. The information you find on these Web sites may be biased. It is safer not to trust this information.

Do not trust information that you find on personal Web sites, blogs, and social media sites such as YouTube, Instagram, and Pinterest. These are personal sources and could also contain opinions and contain biased or false information.

RESEARCH TIP!

Never enter your e-mail address, name, age, or other information on a Web site before asking a trusted adult.

If you are unsure about a Web site, ask an adult to take a look at it with you.

Some people pay to have their Web sites appear when search engines do certain searches. For example, you might do a search for the word "computer." An advertisement for the site of a company that sells computers may appear on the screen when you do that search. Ads for Web sites like these are usually in a shaded box or placed to the side of the other links found by the search engine. Do not click on those ads. You may not be able to trust the information you find on those Web sites.

Become an Expert Researcher

The more research you do online, the better you will get at finding what you need quickly. One way to keep track of the information you find and the Web site you found it on is by printing the Web pages you use. When you write your report, always list the addresses of the Web pages from which you got your information. Do not copy text from a Web site word for word. If you copy words from a site exactly, you are stealing

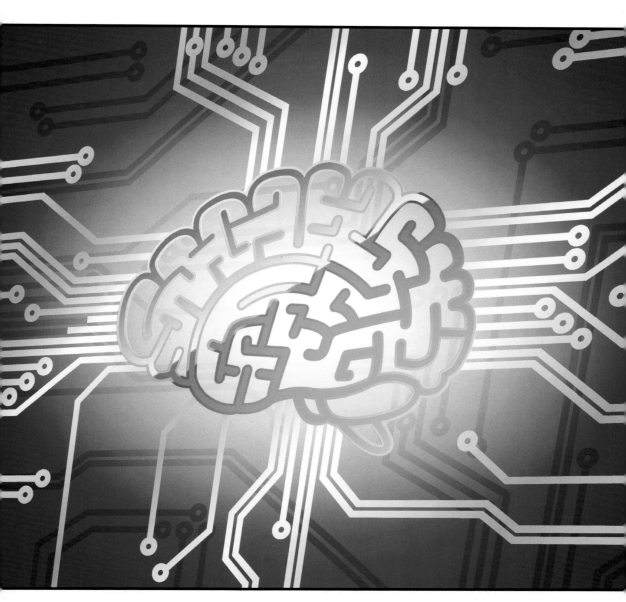

The more Internet research you do, the better you will become at finding what you need.

Knowing how to do research online is very important for doing schoolwork. It is also a good way to learn about fun stuff!

someone else's work. Instead, write your report in your own words.

When you research online, stay focused on your research. Turn off your phone, and don't click on links that take you away from the information you are looking for. Do take breaks every hour.

The Internet is a great source of information. Knowing how to do Internet research will help you in school and in life. If you are ready to learn, get ready to search!

RESEARCH TIP!

To get comfortable doing online research, start with a topic you know about, such as your favorite singer, animal, sport, or author.

Learn More

Books

Coleman, Miriam. ***Share It: Using Digital Tools and Media.*** New York: Rosen Publishing Group, 2012.

Endsley, Kezia. ***How to Do Great Research Online***. New York: Cavendish Square Publishing, 2015.

McKenzie, Precious. ***Library Skills and Internet Research.*** Vero Beach, Fla.: Rourke Publishing Group, 2014.

St. John, Amanda. ***How to Find Information Online.*** North Mankato, Minn.: The Child's World, 2012.

Web Sites

si.edu/kids

Smithsonian Institute children's research Web site with links to all Smithsonian museums.

kids.nationalgeographic.com

Provides reliable information to young researchers on a wide variety of topics.

kidsclick.org

Search engine designed by librarians for children.

Index

A

advertisements, 25

American Museum of Natural History, 16, 20, 21

B

blogs, 11, 22

bookmark, 13

E

encyclopedias, 18, 19

experts, 11, 17, 19

F

facts, 7, 10, 11

Field Museum, 17

G

Google, 12

H

homework, 18

K

keywords, 13, 14

Kid Click, 12

L

libraries, 18

links, 18, 25, 29

N

NASA, 16

news, 8

P

preferences, 12

R

reports, 7, 10, 26, 29

S

search engines, 12, 13, 25

Smithsonian Institute, 16

sources, 11, 16, 21, 29

subscriptions, 18

W

White House, 9

World Wide Web, 8

Published in 2016 by Enslow Publishing, LLC.
101 W. 23rd Street, Suite 240, New York, NY 10011

Library of Congress Cataloging-in-Publication Data
Yearling, Tricia.
 How do I find information online? / Tricia Yearling.
    pages cm. — (Online smarts)
 Includes bibliographical references and index.
ISBN 978-0-7660-6839-1 (library binding)
ISBN 978-0-7660-6837-7 (pbk.)
ISBN 978-0-7660-6838-4 (6-pack)
1. Internet searching—Juvenile literature. I. Title.
ZA4230.Y43 2015
025.0425—dc23
                         2015007005

Printed in the United States of America

To Our Readers: We have done our best to make sure all Web sites in this book were active and
appropriate when we went to press. However, the author and the publisher have no control over
and assume no liability for the material available on those Web sites or on any Web sites they may
link to. Any comments or suggestions can be sent by e-mail to customerservice@enslow.com.

Photo Credits: Chris Bernard/E+/Getty Images, p. 6; damircudic/E+/Getty Images, p. 28; Elena
Kalistratova/iStock/Thinkstock (chapter opener and front and back matter); Fuse/Getty Images,
p. 15; Ivcandy/Digital Vision Vectors, p. 27; Katrina Wittkamp/Digital Vision/Getty Images,
p. 10; Keith Brofsky/Uppercut Images/Getty, p. 24; Mark Edward Atkinson/Blend Images/Getty
Images, p. 19; Purestock/Thinkstock (series logo), p. 3; RubAn Hidalgo/E+/Getty Images, p. 23;
Shouoshu/iStock/Thinkstock (digital background), p. 3; Sashatigar/iStock/Thinkstock (doodle
art on contents page and fact boxes); Sirikornt/iStock/Thinkstock (boy), p. 3; Syda Productions/
Shutterstock, p. 5.

Cover Credits: Purestock/Thinkstock (series logo); Shouoshu/iStock/Thinkstock (digital
background); Sirikornt/iStock/Thinkstock (boy).